THE
New Testament
from A-Z

A Spirited
Romp through
the Christian
Scriptures

Drawings and Text by
JAY SIDEBOTHAM

MOREHOUSE PUBLISHING
An imprint of Church Publishing Incorporated
Harrisburg—New York

With love,
to my Father Jack

Morehouse Publishing, 4775 Linglestown Road,
        Harrisburg, PA 17105
Morehouse Publishing, 445 Fifth Avenue,
    New York, NY 10016
Morehouse Publishing is an imprint of Church
        Publishing Incorporated.

Cover art: Jay Sidebotham
Cover design: Corey Kent

Library of Congress Cataloging-in-Publication Data

Sidebotham, Jay.
    The New Testament from A-Z : a spirited romp through
the Christian scriptures / drawings and text by Jay
Sidebotham.
        p.   cm.
    ISBN-13: 978-0-8192-2274-9 (pbk.)
    1. Bible. N.T.—Dictionaries. I. Title.
BS2312.S53 2007
225.3—dc22

                                        2007019732
            Printed in the United States of America
            07 08 09 10 11 12   10 9 8 7 6 5 4 3 2 1

INTRODUCTION

In my ministry as a parish priest, people often ask how to begin to study the Bible. The question is often asked in such a way that such study sounds like an overwhelming task, like redirecting the course of the Mississippi River, or building a pyramid. Many people have not done any Bible study since their last Sunday school classes, which may have been decades ago. It can be tough to know where to begin. Some courageous pilgrims begin with Genesis, only to find themselves bogged down somewhere in Leviticus. Wise Christians have recommended a variety of ways to access the scriptures, like starting with the Psalms, or beginning with the Gospel of Mark, the earliest and briefest of the four gospels.

I don't pretend to know the best way to begin, but I do know that spiritual growth will follow engagement with these holy pages. And so, in my ministry, I've felt a calling to simply get people started, to get people interested. In that spirit, I offer this small book. It includes twenty-six entries, one for each letter of the alphabet. Each entry highlights a character or concept found in the twenty-seven books of the New Testament, suggests some Bible passages to explore, and invites the reader to think about how the New Testament can go to work in the world today. The drawings and rhymes are simple. They're meant to bring a smile. And along the way, they're meant to draw us into some newer or deeper engagement with scripture, some new insight into our faith, because one can discover life in these pages, the life that Jesus came to bring. Enjoy.

The Rev. Jay Sidebotham

ABCDEFGHIJKLMNOPQRSTUVWXYZ

A is for Andrew
Whose living was fishin'
'Til he hooked up with Jesus
And landed a mission.

Andrew, the brother of Simon Peter, was one of the first disciples. Like other disciples, Andrew was a fisherman by trade. One might wonder how successful these disciples were at their jobs. We never hear that they can catch any fish without Jesus' help. In Matthew's gospel (find the story in Matthew 4:18–20), Peter and Andrew immediately drop their nets and follow when Jesus calls them. In John's gospel (John 1:20–42), Andrew discovers Jesus and then tells his brother Peter that Jesus is worth following. Read about Andrew and think about who you can invite to meet Jesus, by what you say and by what you do.

A**B**CDEFGHIJKLMNOPQRSTUVWXYZ

B is for Barnabas,
Traveled with Paul
Which some might consider
A really tough call.

We are introduced to Barnabas in the book of Acts (read Acts 9). He paved the way for St. Paul to become part of the church, reassuring the first Christians that the man who had been persecuting them was now on their side. As Paul's journeys began, Barnabas traveled with him. The experience was probably neither dull nor easy. Paul relied on traveling companions like Barnabas, whose name means "son of encouragement." As they traveled, Barnabas clearly was challenged to live into his name. Read about Barnabas and think about how, in the course of your journey, you can be a source of encouragement to those with whom you travel, even and especially when the going gets rough.

C is Cornelius,
A soldier from Rome,
Who shows that outsiders
Can call the church home.

11

You can read about Cornelius in the book of Acts (chapter 10). He was a Roman soldier, a man in charge, a boss. One day he was told by an angel to find St. Peter. About the same time, St. Peter had a vision that led him to conclude that the newly formed Christian community would be open not only to Jewish people, but also to Gentiles, like Cornelius. This radical notion, hard for Peter to embrace, had to be driven home by a remarkable vision that he saw three times. Cornelius was welcomed into the early church, opening a door that had formerly been shut to him. Read his story and think about how the good news of inclusion can be applied today. God's love is always broader than we expect.

ABC**D**EFGHIJKLMNOPQRSTUVWXYZ

D is for doubting
Thomas, whose story
was "Show me." One wonders
Was he from Missouri?

You could say that Thomas gets a bad rap. How would you like to go down in history as a doubter? He was a loyal disciple with a penchant for direct and pointed questions. He was committed to following Jesus. We can imagine that after Jesus' death he was deeply disappointed. When he missed one of the disciples' meetings, those in attendance told him they'd seen the risen Lord. It's not surprising that Thomas was skeptical. He wouldn't be fooled again. At their next gathering, with Thomas present, Jesus appeared again. The appearance led Thomas from doubt to faith. We tell Thomas's story (find it in John 20) because doubt and faith are always intertwined. Know that it's okay to bring your doubts.

ABCD**E**FGHIJKLMNOPQRSTUVWXYZ

E is for Eutychus,
His story confirmin'
The perils of falling
Asleep in a sermon

ABCD**E**FGHIJKLMNOPQRSTUVWXYZ

Eutychus was a young man who showed up to hear St. Paul preaching. It was a sell-out crowd—the only seat available was on the window sill. Clearly, Paul was a fine preacher, though perhaps he could have used an editor. He preached on and on that night. The sermon was so long, in fact, that Eutychus dozed off and tumbled out the window. That caused Paul to bring the sermon in for a landing. He found Eutychus, fatally wounded on the sidewalk. Through God's power, Paul brought the young man back to life. We don't hear about Eutychus again, but we can imagine that he didn't nod off in church anymore. Read his story in Acts 20. And try to stay awake during the sermon. Preachers appreciate it.

ABCDE**F**GHIJKLMNOPQRSTUVWXYZ

F is for Felix
Who put Paul on trial
Then left him in prison
For quite a long while.

ABCDE**F**GHIJKLMNOPQRSTUVWXYZ

Of all the shortcomings folks might assign to St. Paul, shyness was not one of them. He was so convinced of the gospel to which he had committed his life that he fearlessly brought it before the leaders of his day. One of those leaders was King Felix. As recorded in Acts 24, Paul explained the Christian faith to Felix and his wife. Paul used the opportunity not to seek his own freedom, but to see if he could convince Felix to become a Christian too. Felix was mildly interested, but didn't take the leap of faith. He said he'd think about it, and while he was doing that, he left Paul in prison. It makes you wonder whether you're missing a message given by God, a message right in front of you.

G

ABCDEF**G**HIJKLMNOPQRSTUVWXYZ

G are Galatians
Who made St. Paul sore
By preaching the gospel
and then adding more.

27

ABCDEF**G**HIJKLMNOPQRSTUVWXYZ

The Galatians were Christians living in the region we refer to as Asia Minor, today known as Turkey. When Paul wrote these Christians in the letter preserved in the New Testament, he talked turkey. He let them have it. He was as mad as we ever see him, mad because these Christians had set up litmus tests that added to the gospel of grace in which Paul believed so strongly. They wanted Gentile Christians to go through Jewish rites of initiation, but Paul would have none of it. In his letter, Paul presents a radical vision of the church, one we have never been able to fully realize. He said: In Christ "there is no longer Jew or Greek, . . . slave or free, . . . male or female" (Galatians 3:28). Read the letter to the Galatians. Then ask yourself how you can live out its vision today.

H

ABCDEFG**H**IJKLMNOPQRSTUVWXYZ

H is for Hypocrites
Sparked Jesus' teaching
By failing to practice
The things they were preaching.

In response to the common complaint that organized religion is just an assembly of hypocrites, the most one can say in response is: "Guilty as charged." Jesus knew that, as he looked around at the religious people of his day. Nothing seemed to make him angrier than people who did not practice what they preached, people who demanded greater religious observance from others than they were willing to observe themselves. It's been said Jesus came to comfort the afflicted and afflict the comfortable. Among those most afflicted then would be the ones he called hypocrites. Read some of what he has to say about them in Matthew's gospel, for instance in Matthew 5. It's not exactly Jesus meek and mild.

I

ABCDEFGH**I**JKLMNOPQRSTUVWXYZ

I is Iscariot,
Judas's last name.
Betrayal becoming
His main claim to fame.

You don't run across many children named Judas, let alone Iscariot. His name lives in infamy, and reminds us that one of the deepest pains in Jesus' life was the sting of betrayal. We don't know a lot about Judas. One of the gospels reports that he handled the money for the disciples—one of the ways people still get in trouble in church. It's not clear whether he was in control of his actions, or whether he was possessed in such a way that he couldn't help. But Luke tells us he ended up regretting what he had done, and that he didn't wait long enough to experience grace and forgiveness. In the end, he took his own life. Read how his story ends in Acts 1.

ABCDEFGHI**J**KLMNOPQRSTUVWXYZ

J is for Jesus
The heart of our story
Whose hour on the cross
Was his hour of glory.

At the center of the New Testament stands Jesus, whose singular life is depicted in the four gospels. The Gospel of John simply could not do it. From its earliest chapters, it describes Jesus proceeding toward his "hour of glory." Ironically, that hour turns out to be the time Jesus spends on the cross. There's not much that would seem glorious in this means of execution, but it is the place where the meaning of Jesus' name ("God saves") is revealed. When you think about it, that expression of love is something truly glorious. Read about this hour of glory in the Gospel of John, chapters 18–20. Give thanks for the love revealed in this hour.

ABCDEFGHIJ**K**LMNOPQRSTUVWXYZ

K is the kingdom
That Jesus brought in
The good news he offered:
Let God's reign begin.

From the beginning of the Gospel of Mark, the earliest of the four gospels, we read that Jesus arrived to announce that the kingdom of God was at hand. It's a theme that surfaces in each of the gospels, but what kind of king are we talking about? Jesus said that the kingdom was beyond us, that it was coming. He also said that it was within each one of us. When asked by Pilate about his kingdom, Jesus explained that his kingdom was not of this world. John's gospel reports that the sign posted at the top of the cross said that Jesus was a king. His kingdom was one with a different kind of power, the power of love and grace and forgiveness. How can you put that power to work in the world?

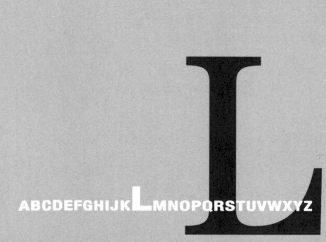

ABCDEFGHIJK**L**MNOPQRSTUVWXYZ

L is for Lazarus
Could not have been deader
'til Jesus showed up
And made him feel better.

The gospels report that Jesus, like all of us, had a few special friends, among whom we count Mary, Martha, and Lazarus. One day in his travels, Jesus got the news that Lazarus was sick, and then that he had died. Jesus arrives to comfort his friends Mary and Martha, but they wonder what took him so long. Touched by their grief, the shortest verse in the Bible conveys Jesus' compassion. In the King James Version, it reads: "Jesus wept." But that's not the end of the story. Jesus goes to the tomb and calls Lazarus forward. The miracle is one of the signs found in John's gospel, a sign indicating who Jesus is. Read the story in John 11, and think about how Jesus brings new life.

M

ABCDEFGHIJKL**M**NOPQRSTUVWXYZ

M is for Mary
Whose faithful reply
To newsbreaking angel was
"Lord, here am I."

When you think about it, there are all kinds of answers Mary could have given the angel. When that heavenly messenger appeared and told her that by the power of the Holy Spirit she would have a child, she could have said "Thanks but no thanks." Like most folks who have close encounters of the angelic kind, Mary responded with fear. But Mary chose to say yes. That simple nod changed the world. Read her story in the first two chapters of Luke. Thank God for that brave, faithful young woman. Where do you have opportunity to be so courageous?

N

ABCDEFGHIJKLM**N**OPQRSTUVWXYZ

N, Nicodemus,
A scholarly man
Who wondered how old folks
Can be born again

The original "Nick at Nite." Nicodemus, an afflu-
ent, educated leader, made his way after hours to
meet Jesus. Read his story told in John 3. It's
the story of a seeker. Maybe he came late at
night because he was really busy. Maybe he was
afraid of being seen with Jesus. For whatever
reason, he showed up, loaded with questions.
In the course of the conversation, Jesus told
Nicodemus he needed to be "born again."
Nicodemus may have left with more questions
than he arrived with, but he surfaces again, later
in the gospel, as one who spoke up for Jesus, and
one who helped bury Jesus with dignity. How
might your journey be like his? What are you
seeking?

ABCDEFGHIJKLMN**O**PQRSTUVWXYZ

O is Onesimus
Proof crime can pay
He met Paul in prison
And soon found the way.

ABCDEFGHIJKLMN**O**PQRSTUVWXYZ

The brief letter of Philemon tells the story of Onesimus, a young man Paul met while they were both imprisoned. Paul used every available opportunity to share his faith. As Paul's prison mate, Onesimus found faith and turned his life around. In turn, Paul went to bat for him, writing what amounts to a scriptural letter of recommendation. Read his story in this succinct, one-chapter letter. Don't blink. You'll miss it. (You may need the table of contents to find it.) Think about how you can put in a good word for someone you know, especially someone who may have messed up at some point. Aren't we all in that category?

P

ABCDEFGHIJKLMNO**P**QRSTUVWXYZ

P is for Prodigal
Son who gives voice
To news that there's hope
If you've made a bad choice.

We owe thanks to St. Luke for preserving the story of the Prodigal Son. It's a great illustration of the good news that even when we get off track, there's a way to come home. The story is certainly about a young man who sows wild oats and ends up feeding sows. It's also about sibling rivalry, good son and bad son on a collision course. But bottom line, it's a story of a gracious, embracing, forgiving parent who sees a lost and misguided child off in the distance, runs down the driveway and throws his arms around the kid before the young man has a chance to recite his speech of apology. Read this classic story in Luke, chapter 15, and imagine God embracing you with that great and deep and forgiving love.

ABCDEFGHIJKLMNOP**Q**RSTUVWXYZ

Q

Q is the question
Which Pilate supplied
He asked: What is Truth?
Jesus gave no reply.

ABCDEFGHIJKLMNOP**Q**RSTUVWXYZ

The Gospel of John lets us eavesdrop on the exchange between Jesus and Pilate. Jesus' life hangs in the balance. Pilate, clearly used to being in charge, seems unnerved by this non-anxious stranger unthreatened by his power. Their encounter ends as they get into a discussion about the nature of truth. Pilate is left asking the question: What is truth? It's a reminder that sometimes a question suggests more than an answer. What questions do you bring?

ABCDEFGHIJKLMNOPQ**R**STUVWXYZ

R is for Rhoda
Who heard Peter knock
When sprung from the prison
She thought: Peter you rock.

Read about Rhoda in Acts, chapter 12. The early Christians had gathered in secret, anxious because their leader, Peter, had been imprisoned. Persecution was in the air, so perhaps they were frightened when a knock came at the door. A young woman, Rhoda, is sent to answer. She opens the door warily, and sees Peter, who'd been delivered from prison by an angel. In her excitement, she runs to tell her friends. Meanwhile, she leaves Peter outside the door. Eventually, they welcome Peter in, and celebrate one more example of the way that God was guiding the church as it was getting off the ground.

S

ABCDEFGHIJKLMNOPQR**S**TUVWXYZ

S is Samaritan
The one we call good
We all could use a few
In our own neighborhood.

Thanks to St. Luke, we know what has come to be known as the story of the Good Samaritan, told in Luke 10. To Luke's readers, such a title might be an oxymoron. Could anything good come from a Samaritan? Yet this story of mercy suggests a broad and hopeful definition of neighborhood. It offers great opportunity to think about how we can behave as neighbors, how the opportunities for neighborliness surround us. Who do you need to see as a neighbor today? Who is that person in your path? Where can you show mercy, which, according to Jesus, is an action that defines a real neighbor?

ABCDEFGHIJKLMNOPQRS**T**UVWXYZ

T is for Timothy
Paul's protege
Who heard that his
Youthfulness got in the way

We read about Timothy in several places in
the New Testament, including in two letters
attributed to St. Paul, letters of instruction and
encouragement to a young companion. Paul was
eager to help Timothy in his journey of faith,
supporting him in his work. Apparently, from
time to time, people thought Timothy was too
young to be worth all the attention. St. Paul says
don't let anyone look down on you because
you're young. It's a reminder of a message told
throughout the bible, that God is able to work in
and through unlikely folks. Like us.

U

ABCDEFGHIJKLMNOPQRST**U**VWXYZ

U, upper room
Where disciples last noshed
Bread and wine blessed and broke
Later on, feet got washed.

Sometimes the most important things a person can say come when that person says goodbye. That may be the case when it comes to Jesus' conversation with his disciples at the Last Supper, which took place in the upper room. In that space, Jesus gave a new commandment, the commandment to love one another. In that room, he instituted the meal of bread and wine in remembrance of him. As the disciples gathered, Jesus promised to send the Holy Spirit, and he shared the news that he was leaving to prepare a place for the disciples. Where would we be without that upper room? Read the lengthiest version of Jesus' farewell address in John's gospel (chapters 13–18). Picture yourself in that room.

V

ABCDEFGHIJKLMNOPQRSTU**V**WXYZ

V is for vineyards
Symbolic places
That Jesus used often
To tell of God's graces.

When Jesus told stories, he used images familiar to the people he addressed. One of his favorite images was the vineyard, not only an image familiar in those surroundings, but a persistent image in the Hebrew Scriptures. Jesus compared God's reign, God's kingdom to the operation of a vineyard. In the metaphor, disciples work in that vineyard, accomplishing God's purposes, and occasionally ignoring the person who runs the vineyard, just the way we occasionally ignore God our creator. Who knows what his imagery would be these days: office cubicles? An assembly line? Read about the vineyard in Matthew 20, and think about how you do the work of the creator.

W

ABCDEFGHIJKLMNOPQRSTUV**W**XYZ

W, the Wise Men
Astrology whizzes
They said: Let the star show
exactly where Jesus is.

We don't know much about these ancient near easterners, but we know they were wise enough to search for a new guiding light. In the second chapter of his gospel, Matthew tells this story of wise men who came from the East, following an unusual star in the sky, a star that led them to Jesus. When they finally arrived at the place where the child was, they worshiped him. It was an epiphany. It's been said that wise men (and women) still seek the Christ child. Use this story of the magi to think about what you are looking for in life. Is there a star guiding you to Jesus?

ABCDEFGHIJKLMNOPQRSTUVW**X**YZ

X, the Greek letter
Referred to as Chi. A
Start to word: Christ
In Hebrew: Messiah

What's in a name? It looks like an "X" to us, but it really is the Greek letter "chi" (rhymes with "guy"), the first letter of the word "Christ," meaning "the anointed one." In Hebrew, the word is "Messiah." The letter then points us to the promise that God would send a savior to come among us. We celebrate in Jesus the arrival of the one promised for a long time.

Y

ABCDEFGHIJKLMNOPQRSTUVWX**Y**z

Y is for youngsters
Who Jesus drew near
Adults said: "Keep quiet!"
Jesus: "Come here."

Jesus had a special place in his heart for children. On one occasion when Jesus was talking to a crowd (see Mark 10), the young people present were doing what young people do: they were making noise. Adults tried to shut them up, but Jesus called the children front and center. He took the youngsters in his arms and blessed them, and suggested to the adults that these young people understood something about the kingdom of heaven that adults were missing. It's not entirely clear what he meant, but it may have something to do with a spirit of openness to God's work. The psalmist tells us that children are a gift from the Lord (Psalm 127). Jesus knew that.

ABCDEFGHIJKLMNOPQRSTUVWXY**Z**

Z is Zacchaeus
As gospels report
He longed to see Jesus
But alas came up short

Zaccheus didn't have many friends, but tax collectors have never won any popularity contests. Working for the Roman occupiers, he charged his own people more than they actually owed. It should not have been surprising to him that he ended up having dinner by himself. On the day when Jesus came to town, this vertically challenged tax collector was so down, he could only go up. He climbed a tree to get a look at Jesus. Read his story in Luke 19. See how Zaccheus is changed after he meets Jesus. How have you changed by an encounter with Jesus?